La Porte County Public Library
La Porte, Indiana

D1221401

IF YOU WERE A KID AT THE
Iditarod

BY JOSH GREGORY • ILLUSTRATED BY KELLY KENNEDY

CHILDREN'S PRESS® An Imprint of Scholastic Inc.

Content Consultant
Danny Seavey, three-time Iditarod musher

NOTE TO THE READER, PARENT, LIBRARIAN, AND TEACHER: This book combines a historical fiction
narrative with nonfiction fact boxes. While all the nonfiction fact boxes are historically accurate
and true, the fiction comes solely from the imaginations of the author and illustrator.

Photos ©:4: Ray Bulson/Getty Images; 9: Chase Swift/Getty Images; 11: patrisyu/iStockphoto; 13: ZUMA
Press, Inc./Alamy Images; 15: Jeff Schultz/age fotostock; 17: Jim Kuhl/Getty Images; 19: Bill Roth/
Anchorage Daily News/MCT via Getty Images; 21: ZUMA Press, Inc./Alamy Images; 23: Ray Bulson/
Media Bakery; 25: Jeff Schultz/age fotostock; 27: Loren Holmes/Adn/ZUMA Press/Newscom.

Library of Congress Cataloging-in-Publication Data
Names: Gregory, Josh, author. | Kennedy, Kelly (Illustrator), illustrator.
Title: If you were a kid at the Iditarod / by Josh Gregory ; illustrated by Kelly Kennedy.
Description: New York, NY : Children's Press, an imprint of Scholastic Inc.,
2018. | Series: If you were a kid | Includes bibliographical references and index.
Identifiers: LCCN 2017032486 | ISBN 9780531232132 (library binding) | ISBN 9780531243114 (pbk.)
Subjects: LCSH: Iditarod (Race)—Juvenile literature. | Sled dog racing—Alaska—Juvenile literature.
Classification: LCC SF440.15 .G74 2018 | DDC 798.8/309798—dc23
LC record available at https://lccn.loc.gov/2017032486

No part of this publication may be reproduced in whole or in part, or stored in a retrieval system, or transmitted in any form or
by any means, electronic, mechanical, photocopying, recording, or otherwise, without written permission of the publisher. For
information regarding permission, write to Scholastic Inc., Attention: Permissions Department, 557 Broadway, New York, NY 10012.
© 2018 Scholastic Inc.

All rights reserved. Published in 2018 by Children's Press, an imprint of Scholastic Inc.
Printed in North Mankato, MN, USA 113

SCHOLASTIC, CHILDREN'S PRESS, and associated logos are trademarks and/or registered trademarks of Scholastic Inc.

Scholastic Inc., 557 Broadway, New York, NY 10012
1 2 3 4 5 6 7 8 9 10 R 27 26 25 24 23 22 21 20 19 18

TABLE OF CONTENTS

Musher

A full Iditarod racing team consists of a musher and about 16 dogs. The dogs pull the musher on a sled packed with gear and supplies.

Sled, with supplies packed

Dog coats

Dog booties

4

A Race Like No Other

Each year in early March, Alaska holds its biggest, most thrilling sporting event: the Iditarod Trail Sled Dog Race. Dozens of the world's top **mushers** gather in Alaska's biggest city, Anchorage. They bring their teams of specially trained sled dogs. Soon, they will set off on an epic race across the state's rugged wilderness. Riding on sleds behind their hardworking dogs, they will cross more than 900 miles (1,448 kilometers) of rough **terrain**. The weather will be cold and snowy. The journey will take more than eight days for even the fastest teams. Imagine you were a kid in Alaska during the Iditarod. You would get an up-close look at this one-of-a-kind event!

Turn the page to set off on an amazing adventure through the Alaskan wilderness! You will find out what it takes to make it to the end of the Iditarod trail.

Meet Maggie!

Maggie Williams lives with her family in a small Alaskan town. Mushing is a big part of their lives. Maggie's dad used to race in the Iditarod every year. Now the family runs a business that takes people on sled dog tours and gives mushing lessons. This year, they are getting back into the big race. Maggie's older sister, Laura, has been training for several years. Now Laura is going to compete in the Iditarod for the first time . . .

Meet Alex!

Alex is Maggie's cousin. He lives in Florida and is visiting Alaska to see the race. His cousins visit him in Florida almost every year. But this is his first time in Alaska. He has never seen snow before! Alex is a little worried that the weather will be too cold for him. Still, hanging out with Maggie will be fun. So will cheering on Laura in the race . . .

Alex set his bags down in the guest room. He was excited to be in Alaska. But he couldn't stop shivering.

"Come on," Maggie said. "I'll give you a tour. You can even meet the dogs!"

"I don't know if I'm ready to go back outside," Alex replied. "I'm freezing just from walking between the car and the house."

Maggie rolled her eyes and handed him a heavy coat. Then she grabbed his arm and led him to the door.

A BRIEF HISTORY OF MUSHING

People have used sled dogs to get around in snowy areas for thousands of years. This way of traveling has a rich history in Alaska. It was once the only way to get to many parts of the state. This was before airplanes or snowmobiles. In the 20th century, Alaskans began holding dog sled races. It was a way to honor their past. This tradition has continued. The Iditarod and other races are held around the state every year.

The first Iditarod Trail Sled Dog Race was held in 1973.

IDITAROD
National Historic Trail ·

Mile 0
Seward · Alaska
★ ★ ★ ★ ★
938 miles to Nome

Maggie took Alex to the dog **kennels**. She led him from one dog to the next. She stopped near a dog with black fur and blue eyes.

"This is Shadow," she said, petting the dog. "He's my favorite. I've helped raise him since he was a puppy. He's still young, but he's very fast."

She walked over to another dog with red and white fur. "This is Max," she said. "He's the lead dog of Laura's team."

Alex laughed as Shadow licked his face. "I can't wait to see them run," he said.

MEET THE TEAM

An Iditarod team usually has 16 dogs. Some have special roles to play. One or two lead dogs run at the front of the group. They have to be able to react quickly to obstacles. Behind the lead dogs are swing dogs. They help the team turn left or right. The dogs right in front of the sled are called wheel dogs. They help steer the sled itself. All the other dogs are simply called team dogs. They add speed and power to the team.

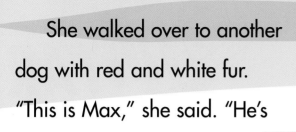

Only northern breed dogs are allowed to race in the Iditarod. These dogs have warm, thick fur. The most common types are Alaskan huskies and Siberian huskies.

The whole family went to Anchorage on Saturday morning. The race's **ceremonial** start was this day. It wasn't the real race. It was a day people could get a close look at the teams. The real race would start the next day. Crowds of excited spectators lined the city streets. Alex shivered as he pointed toward the starting line. "There's Laura," he said. "The mushers and their dogs look so cool!"

One by one, the mushers started racing down the street. They took off a couple of minutes apart. As Laura passed by, she high-fived Alex and Maggie from her sled.

FROM ANCHORAGE TO NOME

Each year, the Iditarod kicks off in Anchorage. Huge crowds gather to watch the mushers race for 11 miles (18 km). This part of the race does not count toward a team's final time. Instead, the race is restarted the next day. The restart takes place in either Willow or Fairbanks, depending on weather. Teams then follow a series of more than 20 **checkpoints** from the restart location to the finish line in Nome.

An Iditarod team can start with up to 16 dogs. At least five of the dogs must remain when the team crosses the finish line.

NOME

The next afternoon, everyone gathered in the tiny town of Willow. It was time for the real start of the race. The wind was strong, and the snow was falling fast. It formed big piles called snowdrifts.

"Is it always this snowy?" Alex asked. He pulled his hood over his head.

"Actually, no," Maggie replied. "This is pretty crazy weather. It's almost a **blizzard**!"

"I hope the dogs will be up to the challenge," her dad added.

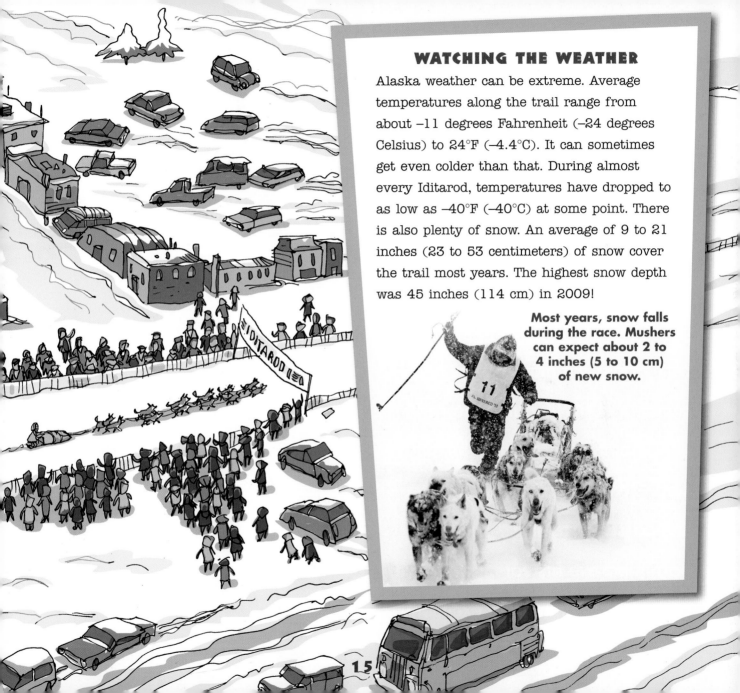

WATCHING THE WEATHER

Alaska weather can be extreme. Average temperatures along the trail range from about −11 degrees Fahrenheit (−24 degrees Celsius) to 24°F (−4.4°C). It can sometimes get even colder than that. During almost every Iditarod, temperatures have dropped to as low as −40°F (−40°C) at some point. There is also plenty of snow. An average of 9 to 21 inches (23 to 53 centimeters) of snow cover the trail most years. The highest snow depth was 45 inches (114 cm) in 2009!

Most years, snow falls during the race. Mushers can expect about 2 to 4 inches (5 to 10 cm) of new snow.

Maggie and Alex were glued to the computer for the next few days. They followed the latest race news closely. They cheered each time Laura reached a checkpoint. Maggie's dad was paying close attention to the race, too. One morning, he had an idea. "Let's fly out to the next checkpoint in my plane," he said. "We could see Laura as she passes through." Alex could hardly believe his ears. "You have an airplane?" he asked excitedly.

FOLLOWING THE ACTION

Watching the Iditarod isn't like watching other sports. You can't go to a stadium to see the race. You can't watch most of it on TV, either. Most fans keep up with the action online. The sleds have **GPS** devices on them. These keep track of the mushers' positions. Live video streams are available at certain points on the trail. The biggest fans try to catch the action in person. They travel to Anchorage, Nome, or even the remote checkpoints.

Fans can ride on a musher's sled during the ceremonial start. But it isn't free. Some pay thousands of dollars to do this.

"Wow," Alex said as he climbed out of the small plane. "This is really the middle of nowhere."

"Yep," Maggie agreed. "The trail goes through some really remote areas."

Maggie's dad led them to a spot where they could see the action. They watched as several mushers passed by.

Finally, Maggie pointed off into the distance. "There she is!" she yelled. But a worried look soon came to her face. "Why is Max running like that?" she asked. "Something is wrong."

RACING STRATEGIES

It takes more than fast dogs to win the Iditarod. Each musher has a **strategy**. The biggest decisions include when to take breaks to eat. Deciding how long to sleep or rest is also important. Another strategy is carrying a few dogs at a time on the sled. The musher can switch which dogs ride in the sled. This lets them rest without stopping.

A musher prepares a meal for his dogs during the 2013 Iditarod.

A **veterinarian** at the checkpoint took a close look at Max. Maggie and Alex watched from a distance.

"I don't think Max is going to be finishing the race," Maggie said.

Her dad nodded. "I think you're right. He'll be coming with us when we leave."

"But what will Laura do without her lead dog?" Alex asked.

"One of the other dogs will have to take over," Maggie answered.

KEEPING DOGS HEALTHY

The Iditarod is difficult for even the strongest, healthiest dogs. Some dogs get injured during the race, just like human athletes might. They also get tired. There are veterinarians at each checkpoint. They inspect the dogs to make sure they are in good shape. Sometimes a dog can't continue the race. Then its musher leaves it behind at the checkpoint. The dog is cared for and flown to either Anchorage or Nome. Then it can rejoin its team after the race.

More than 1,000 dogs compete in the race each year.

21

Maggie and Alex watched as Laura set off on the icy trail.

Alex pointed out that a black dog was leading the team.

"It's Shadow!" Maggie yelled.

"He's an interesting choice for the lead position," said her dad. "He doesn't have Max's experience."

"That's true," Maggie replied. "But I know he can do it!"

RULES OF THE RACE

Mushers must follow a number of rules over the course of the race. They must take regular rest breaks. They also must take three long breaks. One lasts 24 hours. It can be taken at any checkpoint. The other two are eight hours each. They happen at certain points on the trail. Mushers might also stop to sleep outdoors for a couple of hours at a time at other points along the trail, but they try to stay awake as much as possible. Mushers must keep their sleds stocked with certain supplies at all times. These include food, an ax, snowshoes, and a sleeping bag. They also need to have plenty of dog food. And they must carry two sets of booties for each dog's feet.

By packing lightweight supplies, mushers make it easier for their dogs to pull the sled.

A few days later, the whole family went to Nome. They wanted to see the mushers cross the finish line. A little more than eight days had passed. Suddenly, a siren blasted through the town. Alex jumped in surprise.

"What's that?" he yelled.

"Don't worry," Maggie said with a laugh. "That happens whenever a team is close to finishing."

They watched as several teams came rushing into town that afternoon. It was starting to get dark. There was still no sign of Laura.

A PRIZE FOR THE SLOWEST TEAM

Even the fastest teams take more than eight days to complete the Iditarod. For others, the journey can take much longer. The last team to cross the finish line wins a special award. It's called the Red Lantern. The longest time ever recorded was at the first Iditarod in 1973. The Red Lantern winner took more than 32 days to finish.

In 2017, 72 teams entered the race. Only 64 of them finished successfully.

END OF IDITAROD SLED DOG RACE

Finally, the siren rang again. Maggie and Alex started cheering when they recognized Laura. Shadow was at the front of the team. He was running as fast as the wind.

The family rushed to greet Laura as she crossed the finish line.

"You did it!" Maggie shouted as she hugged her sister.

Laura looked tired, but excited. "I'm a long way from first place," Laura replied. "But I'll be back here next year to try again."

"I can't wait to see it," said Alex. "This was so much fun that I stopped noticing how cold it is!"

MASTERS OF MUSHING

Some mushers have achieved amazing things on the Iditarod Trail.

- Lance Mackey set a record. He won the race four times in a row, from 2007 to 2010.
- Rick Swenson has won the race five times. That is more than any other musher.
- Susan Butcher won the race four times. She won in 1986, 1987, 1988, and 1990.
- Dallas Seavey was 25 when he won in 2012. He became the youngest winner in race history. He has won three more times since then.
- Dallas's father, Mitch Seavey, was 57 when he won in 2017. He became the oldest winner in race history.

Dallas Seavey celebrates with his dogs after winning the 2015 Iditarod.

The Iditarod Trail

There are two main routes along the Iditarod Trail.
Each has a number of checkpoints (labeled below)
that teams must pass through along the way.
The race switches between them each year.

Nome
Safety
White Mountain
Golovin
Elim
Koyuk
Shaktoolik
Unalakleet
Kaltag
Nulato
Galena
Ruby
Northern Route
Cripple
Ophir
Takotna
McGrath
Nikolai
Eagle Island
Southern Route
Grayling
Anvik
Shageluk
Iditarod
Rohn
Rainy Pass
Finger Lake
Skwentna
Yentna
Willow
Standard Route
Anchorage

Timeline

1898 The town of Nome is established after gold is discovered there.

1908 A trail is created to make it easier for people to reach Nome. It is named the Iditarod Trail.

1925 A dog named Balto leads a sled team to carry medicine along the trail to Nome. The medicine is needed to help cure an outbreak of a deadly disease in the town.

1967 A short race is held along 9 miles (14.5 km) of the Iditarod Trail.

1973 The first Iditarod Trail Sled Dog Race is held.

1985 Libby Riddles becomes the first woman to win the race.

2017 Mitch Seavey wins the Iditarod with a record time of 8 days, 3 hours, 40 minutes, and 13 seconds.

Words to Know

blizzard (BLIZ-urd) a severe snowstorm with strong winds

ceremonial (ser-uh-MOH-nee-uhl) relating to a formal sequence of events to mark an important occasion

checkpoints (CHEK-poynts) places where something is looked at to learn its condition

GPS (GEE PEE ESS) technology that uses a system of satellites to track something's precise location on Earth; GPS is short for "global positioning system"

kennels (KEN-uhlz) shelters where dogs are kept

mushers (MUH-shurz) people who ride on sleds pulled by teams of dogs

strategy (STRAT-i-jee) a clever plan for winning a race or accomplishing a goal

terrain (tuh-RAYN) an area of land

veterinarian (vet-ur-uh-NAIR-ee-uhn) a doctor who is trained to treat sick animals

Index

ABOUT THE AUTHOR

Josh Gregory is the author of more than 120 books for kids. He has written about everything from animals to technology to history. A graduate of the University of Missouri–Columbia, he currently lives in Chicago, Illinois.

ABOUT THE ILLUSTRATOR

Born and raised in Los Angeles, California, Kelly Kennedy got his start in the animation business doing designs and storyboards at Nickelodeon. Since then, he's drawn and illustrated for a variety of children's books and magazines and is currently working on some of his own stories. When not drawing, he can be found working on his old cars or playing guitar in a bluegrass band.

Visit this Scholastic website for more information about the Iditarod:

www.factsfornow.scholastic.com

Enter the keyword **Iditarod**

32